CONVERSATIONS
WITH THE UNIVERSE

CONVERSATIONS WITH THE UNIVERSE

A COLLECTION OF POETRY BY

K. J. ROBINSON

I am a woman
who once was a girl.
I am a writer
who once believed
she would be the last person
to write
in the whole world.
I am a teacher
who once believed
she had nothing
to share.
I am a dreamer
who once never dared
to have dreams and wishes
because those things
are supposed to be
rare.

No,
I wasn't able
to see her.

But now I do.
Because
now I know
I am a child
of the universe.

CONTENTS

INTRODUCTION

DEAR READER,

Writing has not always been something that came naturally to me. When I was in school I disliked analysing poetry and never would I have guessed that one day, I'd be publishing a book, let alone my own poetry collection.

My writing journey started, quite unexpectedly, last year in March. I was meditating, like every morning, and suddenly I had these words floating around in my head. To have thoughts come up during meditation is nothing extraordinary, but after a while I noticed that these words weren't like my own thoughts. They sounded and felt differently somehow. That's when I became curious and I began to write them down until, to my own surprise, I was sitting in front of pages filled with short poems.

Where did these words come from? What did it all mean? I didn't know. All I knew for sure was that they didn't belong to me, because never before was I able to express myself so eloquently. But soon the answer to these questions popped into my head— *share*.

I knew then that I had to share these words with others. The Universe was sending me an invitation. And I accepted it.

In the past year I learned that the Universe speaks to us all, but the messages are often clouded by our own thoughts and judgement.

Conversations with The Universe explores the possibility that messages from Spirit/Source/Your Higher Self are being transmitted to us everyday, through signs, synchronicities, songs, people we meet and conversations we have and yes, even our own thoughts - all we have to do is listen. This collection of poems will provide you with the wisdom you seek and the peace you need, while offering hope, love, and happiness.

If this book found its way to you, there's a message you need to hear - and it's time for you to tune in and listen. So let this be your invitation to open up your mind to new possibilities and to connect and communicate with the universe.

Many Blessings,

Kim Joanna

A NEW JOURNEY BEGINS

There's rain hiding
within your eyes
and wind flowing
inside your lungs.

There's sun
shining
in your heart
and there's fire
burning
beneath your skin.

There's earth
grounding your feet
and there's water
giving your life
a new, refreshing spin.

But don't forget
the energy
underneath it all;
the stuff
that makes you,
that shapes you,
the stuff
that lets it all
begin.

Words from Beyond

What is going on?
To whom do these words belong?
They are so unlike me.
Could it be my true self
has finally been set free?

Well, this I know for sure
these words,
they almost feel like a cure.
Inspiring me to write
what's hiding deep inside.

My minds been hazy,
always thought I was crazy.
Now that the fog is clearing,
my inner being appearing.

In sheer vibrancy
these words are showing
my inner world,
brightly glowing.

Who you're talking to?

An infinite stream
of love
of light
of well being
of healing
of wisdom
and insight.

Coming through
a vessel
called
your Inner Being.

— The Universe

Existence

Who has put us
upon this earth,
what is the reason
for our birth?

We exist
in clusters
of physical matter,
we live
in a world
dominated by logic
where endless streams of chatter
have become chronic.

We run
in circles, back and forth
further losing track
of our true north.
We lose touch
with our guidance
from deep within,
people try to hide it
by shutting it in.

There is more to us
and our existence;
we need to tune in
in order to find it,
release the resistance
behind it;
only then
the wisdom of the universe
will be there
for our assistance,
but first—
we have to let it in.

I am as bright as day
with the spectrum
of all the colors.
If you want me to,
I can give you
higher powers
by helping you realize
that within you, sleeping,
is the potential to bloom
like a million of flowers.

— The Universe

World of Camouflage

In this world
of camouflage
most don't seem
to really see or grasp
the energy behind it all
but you have the ability
too peek behind
its wall.

The Eternal in Eternity

Where is the eternal
in eternity?
A never-ending universe
existing in certainty.

Compared, our lives seem
insignificant and small.
What a false premise,
for we are important
and tall!

For you, my dear,
you are the universe
in all of its glory.
Each day,
you get to write
your own story.

If you want to thrive,
know there's no perfection in this life.
Embrace the imperfection,
to find the right direction.

Try to listen closely,
'cause your soul is calling boldly.
Urging you to go with the flow.
and then someday soon,
you'll see, you'll glow.

Because striving
for the finish line,
will not make you feel whole.
It's the moment by moment thriving
that makes the journey
cloud nine.

Closets

Why
do you hide yourself
in these closets
of restriction
behind hangers
of personalities
and of beliefs
while
the true you
is collecting dust,
hidden underneath
concealing layers
of fabric
all because
of your own distrust.

Why not
open up the doors
of your being,
express yourself bravely,
act like the kings and queens
of the universe
knowing
who you truly are
and claim what lies
within your genes.

I am a mystery.
I am not defined by what I do or what I have.
I am something that is unfolding.
I am something new with every breath.
I am not the same as yesterday.
I am constantly changing and growing.
I am somebody that is worth getting to know.
I have a story to tell.

There is more to me than what meets the eye
so ask me who I am,
and be prepared to listen.

— The Universe

True Power

Hope and faith
give you power.
It's the universe's shower
of joy, love
and the purest light.

Try it
and you might get to see
your life
can be oh so bright.

Forget the past
and everything that was;
set it aside,
throw it away
for it was never meant to last.

All that counts is now;
within it
your power
to rewrite the past.
Make changes;
live and love
more freely;
express your energy;
be a broadcast
for all things wanted—
yes,
life can really be
this easy.

Divine Guidance

Assistance from a different kind,
another realm of reality.
The universe
always has you on its mind.
Even if your life seems
like a never ending maze.

Consistently offering you guidance
through signs and synchronicities.
Every moment a new chance
to discover
your life
really is
a great dance.

Magic can happen,
you will see
anything you can imagine
could soon be.

Life will still be up and down,
But that's no reason
for you to frown
'cause that's the way
we are shown
what we want and why.
Can't you see,
that that's divine?

Who knows
what the future holds?
Who knows
how our stories will unfold?

You won't find the answer
by searching externally
but rather
by looking within
carefully;
how we talk to ourselves
is how our story gets told—
energetically.

Be Curious

This is
your invitation
to be curious
about yourself.
To be curious
about others.
To be curious
about nature.

There is so much out there.
The joy. The pain.
The highs. The lows.
The wisdom. The healing.
All available
for you.
For all of us.

It will be different for everyone.
It may be obvious. It may be subtle.
Tune in to what feels right.
And be curious
about life.

Intuition

Seeing bits and pieces
and the bigger picture.
Been sensing this coming
for the most part of my life.

All this time I had a feeling
but didn't know
with what I was dealing.

These emotions go much deeper
than I can comprehend.
But maybe there's no need
to intellectually understand.

Choose

You get to choose
if your life's painting
is one of bright colors
or a monochrome diffuse.

Love, light
and harmony
always there,
waiting
for you to be found.

All you have to do
is choose.

You may ask yourself,
what if I fall?
Not considering at all,
what could happen if
things turn out great,
if you jump over the wall
of fear
and don't wait.

And if you need
some more time
before you can proceed,
just know I'll wait for you
in the meantime.

— The Universe

WHAT IS RIGHT NOW
WILL SOON BE PAST

SO MAKE THIS

MOMENT COUNT

FOR IT'S THE MEMORIES
THAT WILL LAST.

Let this day be new

Life's not worth to spend it
condemning or resenting one another.
So many better uses of energy and time,
so why would you bother?

No one is perfect,
we all mess up at times.
The past is the past,
that we might as well choose to forget.
Let's live in the present,
not remembering the days before
so they don't have the power
to cause discontent.

The Now, the only thing that counts.
Forgive others, yourself too,
forget what was, what were
and let this day be new.

A light shining through
the closed doors of your soul;
you may try to hide it
but no matter how much force,
how much you tried to control,
living in alignment
with your true essence
is the only thing
that can make you feel whole.

Life is

like the t-shirt
that you used to wear
everyday
where slowly
the holes start to form
and you try to
patch it up
with a needle
and a thread
but the holes get bigger
still, you don't want
to let go
until I say
"throw that shirt away"
and you say
"you're probably right".

Life is
like your favorite t-shirt
change is inevitable
and one day
you will have to let go,
get a new one,
surrender,
if you ever want
to grow.

Actions over Words

Do you really think
that words do matter,
yes they do,
but there's something stronger.

Do you really think
that people don't notice,
yes they notice,
your actions and how they align
with the words you speak.

Do you really think
you can just sit there,
and yes you could,
but the best things out there
require participation -
tell me, your waiting,
how much longer?

The Universe's Kiss

Is there hope in your life?
'Cause without faith
you might dismiss,
the beauty around you,
the universe's kiss.

Dancing, joyfully
in swirls of light
around your Being.
It's your birthright,
not ever fleeing.

Come with me,
set your heart
free;
allow the love
you're supposed
to be
so you may finally
see
how wonderful
life
can really be.

— The Universe

There are things
no one can see or grasp.
They go beyond
the five senses.
Not to touch or hear,
so how does one define them?
How to make what is felt
seem near?

The answer is simple:
these things are
your opportunity
to feel,
to leave logic aside
just for a little while.

— The Universe

The Calling

You know what to do.
Go after it.
Follow
the calling.

— The Universe

It's Time

It's time
to start listening
to the inner voice within.

It has been trying
to impart a message,
to give you a hint.
An answer
to the questions,
those that in your mind
endlessly spin.

It's time
for you
to pay attention
it's time
to begin.

SEE THE SIGNS

Connect the Dots

I am here
and yet
I am not.
I am everywhere
and anywhere
yet
you can see me not.
I speak to you
every second
of everyday
and yet
you can't hear any sound
so you don't notice, a lot.

Still, my guidance
will prevail,
sent out to you
in masses
until you manage
to set logic aside,
to honor your inner senses—
until you connect
the dots.

— The Universe

Am I going crazy
or am I making sense of it all?
Sometimes it still seems hazy
oh, I really don't want to fall.

My only choice,
to trust my inner voice,
the signs around me,
believe in what I can foresee.

The Secret

Let me tell you
a secret,
said the universe,

the key
to all your dreams
and wishes
lies not
in needing to see it
but instead
in being willing
to believe it
and to feel good
on your journey
until
you meet it.

Another world

Existing within you
another world
called the inner senses.
They speak to you
day and night.
They guide you
from the dark
into the light.

Will you listen
or will you ignore
this other world?
The choice is yours.

Don't be too quick to judge
what is seen around you.
The universe
giving you a nudge—
there are things out there
so much more profound
BUT FIRST
you need to shift your perspective
and stop worrying
so much.

Signs

The answers to your questions
the universe always provides
sometimes you just have
to read between the lines-
have you noticed them,
the signs?

Soul Family

You are not for everyone
and that's a good thing.
All the little intricacies
all your skills, gifts and talents
all that makes you, you.

Who else has that?
No one.

So let this be your sign
that soon you'll find
the right people
who will value you
and with whom
you'll align.

And when there's absolutely
nothing left to do
and all your paths have left confusion
deep inside you
look up at the sky,
no matter if it's day or night,
'cause there's guidance always close by
if you never let your hope
get out of sight.

Fears?
Insecurities?
Traumas?

You don't have
to be brave
and walk through them
in order to heal.

There's a way
around them—
Open your eyes.

— The Universe

Facets of a Soul

The many facets
of a soul

like petals on a flower
like layers of an onion
like the branches of a tree

from all these
individual aspects
making a whole
from these fragments
there are so many worlds to see

the soul knows them
all at once
yet in our awareness
exists only one

the full picture
beyond our senses
not equipped
to look through all these
different lenses

yet still
some may grasp
a little piece of it
here and there

sensing
the unity
that is at our essence,
the unity
that we all inherently
share.

Positive aspects
can be found
in every place
you might be around.

Even if it's
the smallest sound
or something hiding
in the background;
there's still beauty
of great amount.

Simply by choosing
to live your life this way
and you carrying the light
no matter what others say.

No more chase
for external bliss
'cause wherever you are
pure positive energy
follows you
that no one could miss.

For just a minute
pause and breathe,
listen to the thoughts
playing underneath.

Adjust your focus
to the real priority:
your feelings
equal
your energy's currency.

A Message

This melody
that keeps replaying
inside your head
— it is trying to give you a message.

These words
that keep finding you
on billboards, in books
and in conversations
— they are trying to give you a message.

These feelings
that come out of nowhere
but ring true deep within
— they are trying to give you a hint.

It's all guidance
but in order to hear,
truly and undistorted,
one must be willing
to listen.

You are ready
my dear.

— The Universe.

See, that bird
flying in the sky.
And look, the leaves
flowing with the wind.

How the cat
wanders about it's day;
and where once was only grass
now blooms a bed of flowers
that would make for
a beautiful bouquet.

All proof
that nature's beauty
is to be found
in the smallest moments
of every day.

You often ask
"when?"
but haven't you noticed
we always
give you the same answer:
As soon as
you believe
that it is.

Pretty neat
isn't it?

— The Universe

Align

The moment I stopped trying
and went with the stream
it felt like
I stepped into a dream.

All previous strife and struggle
vanished
almost instantly
and my life looked like
it was painted with colors
of a much brighter theme.

Could it really be this easy,
to just go with the flow?
I asked the universe
for a confirming sign
and all I could find
was evidence
from the divine
that the answer
was always with me;

to feel relief
is a helpful clue,
to feel a little better
is all that's needed
for me to align.

Yes.

You wanted to know
the answer
and this
is our reply —

Yes.

— The Universe

THE UNIVERSE SINGS

Within your own being
the universe sings
like the truth
that the leaves outside
are flowing,
like the truth
that the flowers outside
are growing.

Yet,
most do not listen,
afraid to accept
the truth
that they themselves
are the universe
embodied
in physical form.

But
those who dare to listen
only for the smallest
second
will not ever be able
to unhear —
their life
forever
transformed.

It's coming —
the thing
you have been
waiting for
praying for
asking for.
It's almost there.
You can already sense it,
right?
Because you've noticed
all the many signs
that found its way to you.

We hope you're ready
'cause your wildest dreams
are about to come true.

— The Universe

Trust

Deep down
you already know
that it's true.

So why do you still
doubt and worry?
We have been sending
plenty of signs
your way
lately.

We know
you saw them.

Go ahead.
Trust.

— The Universe

BETWEEN WORLDS

Secrets from Yourself

Did you know
you've been keeping
secrets from yourself—
the thoughts
that visit time and time again
and yet
you act as if they don't exist;
the feelings
that keep on coming
and yet
you decide that silent
they should remain;
the impulses
that appear in your gut
and yet
you don't act, you keep them contained.

Creating divisions
that aren't grounded
in reality;
only by keeping secrets
from yourself
you create them,
divisions from your broader self.

Say,
how much longer
will you choose to flee?
How much longer
will it be?

It's okay.
You don't have
to be perfect.
We will work it out
together.

— The Universe

Body

This body
does not feel like mine
as if
in the past, I was one
of a different kind.

Trying to adapt
to this world
of physical reality
feels like
a journey of
figuring out
how to "be"
with no ending—
no finish line.

I am me
and I am not.
I am who I was
but also the futures plot.

Where's the real version of me,
the lifetime I am not hiding,
the one where I feel free—
aren't there supposed to be angels
by my side, guiding?

Parallel Reality

In a parallel reality
not far from here
there's another one
of you and me.
Similar,
yet not the same
and of different quality,
our personality lives
what we in this life
do not want to see.

Body to Soul

I've been at war
with myself
for decades
my body
the battlefield;
I thought I would win,
mind over matter;
I thought I would get
all control
but no—
my mind trapped me
and left me
sore.

The body lead a trump
shutting me down
right at the core.
Until no choice left
but to resign
and surrender
all force
all hate
all fear
all guilt
and the illusion
of having any
external control.

Once blended
by physical reality,
now I know
the body isn't
my enemy
but instead
the door
that leads
to my soul.

What's with all this noise
that we allow
to sweep through
our minds?
Constant voices
and opinions
from all directions
leaving
no time for silence
no space for peace.

But tell me,
how can I know
what the future holds?
My hopes and dreams
will they grow
as each day unfolds?

You get to decide,
the universe whispers,
if you let joy be your guide
the flow
of the rivers of life
will take you
downstream.

Much less struggle
than you ever knew
to let come true
even your wildest dream.

Embrace It All

Feeling sad,
a part of life.
For you cannot be glad,
or really thrive,
if you've never experienced
something bad.

It cannot be one
without the other.
So make peace
and embrace it all:
life, yourself,
yes, even one another.

Rest your past
and forget it
fast.
Tomorrow is your new chance
for your joy
to advance.

If you're missing a place
turn your attention
to the similarities
that exist
between where you are
and where you want to be.
You'll be surprised
how many you can find.

— The Universe

Dandelions

You're free to choose
how you want to see
your growth;
as a garden
full of
annoying weeds
or a meadow of dandelions
with millions of seeds
that can be set free
with just one blow;

every moment of your life
you decide which version
it will be.

Should's and Shouldn't's

My mind is full
of should's and shouldn't's.
This feeling
of constantly running behind,
a never ending push and pull.

In this state of mind
the best I can do
is rest, take a nap,
only then will I be able
to see things much more
aligned
and discover
that with these thoughts
I was just keeping
myself confined.

Never
do something
because you feel like
you should,
you have to,
it would look good,
others will like you
or love you.

Always
do the thing
that makes you feel
more like yourself.

— The Universe

THE PERFECTION WAITING LIST

What's with all this striving
for perfection?
An endless hunt
to reach completion
to reach this destination
where finally
all your desires
fulfilled.

There is no finish line,
this state simply does not exist—
excuse me
for being this blunt
but perfection keeps you
on an eternal
waiting list.

BREATHE IN
to find your inner center.
BREATHE OUT
and release all distemper.

BREATHE IN,
that's how you can find peace
under all conditions;
BREATHE OUT,
that's how you can release
your inhibitions;

then,
all things wanted
MAGICALLY
INCREASE.

Room for All

No words in the world
could ever describe
in sheer accuracy
what it feels like
to love, to hate
to laugh or to cry.

I mean
of course you could try
but why press into tiny boxes
what each of us
uniquely feels and defines?

I believe there's room
for all our perspectives,
for all of us to explore.
Our differences, not our sameness
is what makes life
worth living for.

True Peace

Eventually
they put their arms down
and the others followed.
Both parties realized
peace cannot come
through fighting.
Peace can only exist
when you live by example
with unclenched fists
and surrendering
to the things
you once tried,
so stubbornly,
to resist.

To compare yourself
with another
is like driving
while simultaneously
putting on the brakes—
you won't come very far
if you refuse to see
that beauty lies
within us all.

YOU ALREADY HAVE WHAT IT TAKES.

YOU ALREADY HAVE

WHAT IT TAKES.

Outside the Box

In an open box
with no walls
there's space
for us all
to be
who we want to be
where we can let
all restrictions fall,
be absolutely free.

Yes,
this place
really does exist
you can reach it,
connect with others
who found it too
by focusing
on how you feel;
to be one of the few

who chooses
feeling good
over despair
all you have to do
is shift your focus
and care
about feeling a little better
and be prepared,
your life might turn
upside down.

Do you dare?

— The Universe

Unnecessary
is all that worry
that you continue
to carry.

Totally momentary
the situation you find
yourself standing in
if you would just let it be
and stopped to spread
yourself
so thin.

Destination Chase

The wind carries the leaves
ever so gently
from place to place
until they eventually wither away.

You see,
it's about their journey
not about landing
at any final spot.

The joy is in the journey,
that's what they say
what if there's actually
more truth to this
than not?
Would you then
put an end
to the destination chase
and instead just flow
to the next
best-feeling place?

Are you
living through
your moments
to get to
where you'd rather be
or are you
living in
your moments
because you know
to feel good now,
is the key.

A Treasure Within

Pause
and tune in.
Listen
and take note,
an inner voice
deep within.

Wisdom is inside.
All that's needed
is you.
So take the time,
pay attention
to what's beneath
your wandering mind.

Feeling good
and in the flow.
The only thing you need
and soon you'll know
there's a treasure
of great measure
for you to discover.

In stillness
you can uncover
your brilliance
and even that
of another.

Sometimes
all it takes
is one like-minded person
who just gets you
to change everything.

The way you view life.
The way you think of it.
The way you talk about it.
The way you go through it.

If you haven't met them yet
just know—
they're out there.

And if you have
you know
what we're talking about.

— The Universe

You have
far more control
than you might realize;
within you residing
an eternal stream
of vitality and wellbeing
free flowing energy
to keep you alive
but also for you
to make come true
your wildest dreams.

Joy In The Present

Time running so fast
when you watch it
from present to past.

Still, this is of little account.
The present is where
your focus must be,
if you desire joy
of great amount.

Now I understand,
as clear as day,
divine timing must be at play.

Get clear on what and why,
extract the emotion,
practice sincere devotion.
and don't be shy.

Find waves of ease
washing over you,
knowing all you want,
will soon be yours.

You never fail
to impress us —

STRONG HEART
STRONG SOUL
STRONG FAITH

Don't you see it too?
You've got what it takes.

— The Universe

So you decided to try
and go for it.
But now
you wonder:
Does it have to be perfect?

The thing
you might instead
want to consider:
Does it have to be real?

We know which question
we would answer
with yes.

— The Universe

Twisted Journey

Your journey
may end up
looking different
than you planned.

But that doesn't mean
you don't get to
where you want to be.

Still, you have to understand
life is full
of twists and turns.

There's no way for you to see
the path forward
for miles on end.

But if you're willing
to take the universe's hand,
to walk by faith
and not by sight,
your desired life
will find you
shining, oh, so bright.

CHANGING THE NARRATION

Tonight I am dropping the worry
for all its weight
I can't continue to carry.
Tonight I am picking up the expectation
that all will be well—
I'm changing the narration.

Success

To go from boredom
to feelings of contentment,
that is like success.

To change overwhelm
into a state of hopefulness,
that makes for success.

To shift from feeling fear
into feeling love, gradually;
that surely is success.

Soon
it will all start
to make sense
only
a little more
suspense
until the answers
will reveal themselves
then,
all your worries
will be
past tense.

— The Universe

IF YOU ARE IN NEED OF GUIDANCE

On Purpose

"What's my purpose?
What should be my next goal?
What am I to accomplish?
I'm very sure
there has to be more."

It is true
there is more
but who made you think
that fulfilling your purpose
means to constantly strive
for more?

What's with all the yearning
and the struggling
and the improving?

Didn't you notice
it makes you lose
your sense of presence
and with that
you lose your purpose
because, dear friend,
your purpose
is already being fulfilled
every moment
of every day
just by being alive
and taking another step.

All you have to do is breathe
and trust
and know
that more is already
on it's way to you—
you are worthy of it
simply by existing.

— The Universe

On Inspiration

"Inspiration
it's such a funny thing.
Sometimes it's there.
Sometimes it's gone.
Sometimes it feels
like it's just within reach
but still, it drags on."

Why don't you try
to just follow the lead
of where your intuition
pulls you to.
We promise you
this is the key
to change
the way
your inspiration
comes through.

— The Universe

On Timing

"What time is it?
Is it time to relax and unwind?
Or to take action
and start the climb?
What's next
and where do I need to go?
Please tell me
I really need to know."

We want to tell you
but it truly doesn't matter
as much as you may think
and in the meantime
you miss the point
with each moment
going by
in a blink.

Much more important
than to know
exactly when
is to know
with certainty
your dreams are destined
to begin.

And if you do
you also know
that timing is not for you
to control
instead you relax
and let go
while following the guidance
of your soul.

— The Universe

On Perfection

"Each and every day
I try my best
to be the best version that I can be.
It's exhausting, taking up
all my energy.
But still, I feel the need
for constant improvement.
Please enlighten me,
how can I ever live my life, carefree?"

To your question
the following is the key —
perfection does not exist,
not one perfect person
that of this world
consists.
Do yourself a favor,
stop the yearning
stop the comparing
and start discerning.

We can't say
what's the bigger loss —
to accept life
in all its imperfections
or
to walk the hamster wheel
of perfection
while you deny yourself a life
that is valuable,
honest and real.

For us
it would be too big
a cost.

— The Universe

On Being Angry

What are you
supposed to do
when you get angry?

Scream and shout,
let it show
and get everything out?
Or hide and compress
the emotion
let it build up
and cause even further stress?

Well, you must be able to sense
no good comes if you suppress
any emotions you may feel.
If you don't let them out
at a later time
it will be a much bigger deal.

You are allowed
to be angry.
It is giving you
an opportunity.
Just be aware
of your anger
let it pass through you
and don't let it
consume you.

On Twists and Turns

„Everything is suddenly
upside down
but not in the way
that would make me
frown.
It seems like
things are finally moving,
the change I wanted
now right in front of me.
I just thought it would look different
somehow."

Here's what you
should know:
sometimes
the best things in life
happen unexpectedly
and not in ways
you planned them out.
Forcing things
to go your way
is not
what life is about.
Have you ever considered
that life
not going your way
is your path
to allow the "wow"?

No doubt,
the time for change
is now.

— The Universe

On Passion

Passion is
a divine spark
nestling gently
in between your heart;

a way to live
life more intently,
to let it all be a work of art;
a spirited fire
with flames of inspiration
that can reach into the sky;

a powerful desire
rooted deep inside
the essence of your soul;
tune to it and it may lift you
higher than you've ever been before.

On Being Realistic

"Am I crazy
for believing in my dream
to come through?
The one that would seem
too good to be true?
Am I losing my mind
over these hopes and wishes
that will never be mine?
Or am I right
about interpreting the signs?"

No wish
is ever within you planted
without the possibility
of its reality being granted.
If you ever ask
"was that a sign?"
know your question alone
shows you, it's real.

We are not here
to play games with you.
To help you align,
that was the deal.

— The Universe

On Decisions

"Decisions are not something
to take lightly.
They can be life altering
in an instant.
So how do you go about it
when you can't say,
when you can't choose
between left or right.
Is it A or B?
Please tell me
how to find the light."

These decisions
my dear
are best made
not by counting
pros and cons
but by being still,
allowing your mind
to be just a tiny bit
more clear.

Then you will notice
your heart beating
and that within it
the answer has been hiding
all along.

It knows
where you feel like
you belong.

— The Universe

A LIGHT IN THE DARK

NEVER ALONE

You are not
alone
standing in
the cold
even if it may
seem this way;
the universe
always by your side
ready to unfold;
just turn the next corner

— help is already on the way.

DO NOT
FEAR YOUR
DARKNESS
BECAUSE
WITHOUT IT

YOU
WOULDN'T
BE ABLE
TO KNOW
YOUR LIGHT

Courage

Courage is a little twinkling light
that shines uniquely on its own.
Its presence can be sensed even more
when the sun has already left,
leaving the sky seemingly dark.

But when one looks closely
one will find the endless amount of courage
illuminating the path forward, regardless.

So look back up again,
to find your courage,
your own uniquely, shining light.

Close your eyes and feel the wind in your hair,
listen to the waves crash as they hit the shore,
feel the sand between your toes
and let all your worries wash away.

For a little while, just forget about your troubles
and relax in the moment,
enjoy the peace that surrounds you.

So close your eyes, take it all in:
The beauty of nature
and the serenity of silence.
It's a moment to yourself, a time to reflect
and it's so much better when you know
you're not alone.

— The Universe

All that is needed
is one message,
one spark,
one source of light
within the dark
to let you know
you will be alright—
the universe
is always
by your side.

We Are There

When you feel sad
we send you a hug.

When you feel sick
we send you well being.

When you think less of yourself
we send you our knowledge
of your strength.

When you say you can't
we tell you that you can.

When you act like you don't care
we know that you do.

We are always
right there with you
but in order to notice it
and receive it
you have to be open
to the possibility
that there is more
than the physical world.

— The Universe

This world has so much to offer
if you stop the struggle,
stop being the driving force
and instead choose to view life
from the eyes of source.

Miracles

Miracles exist
after all.

They happen
after months and months
of wait
and countless hours
between hope and worry
and almost crumbling
faith.

But they do happen.
So don't give up now.
I promise you
it will be worth
the wait.

— The Universe

Sadness is a plant
of immense beauty,
no matter it’s shape
or form.
It’s a delicate blossom
with the sole purpose
TO HELP YOU GROW.

And when it all
comes crashing down
and you fear
that you might drown
know that I will catch you
because I
am always around.

— The Universe

Tune Into Love

Tune into
the frequency of love.
You can find it
right there, within your heart.
Always ready, waiting
for you to start.

All that you have to do,
is surrender
all and any struggle.
No bigger secret,
than ease, comfort and flow.
That is all
you need to know.

We think it's funny.

How you hide
your feelings
your thoughts
your truth
inside of yourself
afraid for others to see
afraid for them to judge.

While they keep judging you
no matter what you do
no matter what you feel
no matter what you say.

Don't you think it's time
to be yourself
forget the naysayers
and do life
your way?

— The Universe

I am where I am
and that's okay.
No reason
to feel ashamed
in any way.

Knowing when I'm
in a rainy season
it's for growth
where light is never far—
the universe,
my eternal,
guiding star.

You Are Brave

Ever felt
like giving up?
The fact
that you are still here
reading these words
is proof enough
that you didn't.

You are still here.
You are still trying.
You are so brave.

— The Universe

Just for this moment
I choose to let go
of all the negativity
all the worry
all the overthinking
and the should's and shouldn't's.
I am tired
of constantly rocking
my own boat.

All I want
for this moment
is peace.
All I want is
to float.

Happiness

Happiness is a liquid
that makes life on earth possible.
It's available to everyone
no matter one's circumstances.
It can be found in the most unusual places,
no matter the degree
of light or dark that is present
in any moment.
It gives life its purpose and meaning.
Without it, everything seems bleak
and crushingly pointless.
And the decision to drink its potion
will always remain with you,
forevermore.

Things
have this way
of working out for you—
magically
unexpectedly
suddenly
miraculously
out of the ordinary.

Yet
you never seem
to notice it
while being in
the moment
but always
at some point
when you look back.

Things
are working out
for you
right now.

You've got this.

— The Universe

The Wonders of an Optimist

And your face
radiates
sun-kissed smiles
producing beams of light
for a million miles
even while
it's dark outside
even in
those trying times,
you never fail
to surprise.

Don't stop
believing
singing
dancing
praying
hoping
expecting.

Your dreams—
they're close.

— The Universe

The Sun Will Last

Off in the distance
grey, rumbling clouds;
the storm has passed
and all that's left
are distant sounds;
this phase now being
in your past
allows for new hope
to emerge;
slowly, you're returning
to your wellbeing

and you pray
that this time
the sun will last.

TIME TO TRUST

How Much?

How much
do you dare
to trust
and follow
your intuition?

How much
does it take
for you to say
"I'll follow that feeling"
no matter how crazy
it may seem to others?

How much
time
are you going to spend
contemplating
whether you can
fully trust yourself
even when
there's no backup
that covers?

The universe
is endless,
full of possibilities,
ready to meet you
halfway,
all there's left to do
is for you
to take a leap of faith
each and every
day.

There will always be
those days
where things happen
not as planned,
know that it's ok.

We have to learn
to go with the flow
and trust
that there will always be
a helping hand
but only to the degree
you believe
in the goodness
of yourself;
to the degree
you believe
that for you
things
always work out
alright.

When you're always scared
to take a risk, to go all in,
the result: you will never win.

If you want a difference,
then be ready
to take a chance, 'cause
otherwise you might end up heavy.

Back Up Plan

No matter what you do
please never despair.
We always have
an ace up our sleeves.

We told you
there's always
a back up plan.

Please,
believe.

— The Universe

RELEASE YOUR FEARS
SPEAK THEM OUT
AND WATCH THE MAGIC
IT WILL BRING ABOUT

Honor your inner feelings,
don't surpass them.
They're guidance
from a different realm
each emotion
carrying a different meaning
for you to uncover
to which end
of the spectrum
you are leaning
accepting them
will allow your own
healing.

This and That Can Be True

We don't have a mouth
and yet we talk all the time.

We don't have ears
and yet we listen every day.

We don't have hands
and yet we can touch your soul.

We have no eyes
and yet we see you
everywhere you go.

We make no sound
and yet we speak to you
day in and out.

We are always with you
and yet we are not of physical nature.

But that doesn't mean
we are not as real as
the chair you sit on
or the friend you talk to
or the music you listen to
or the flowers you can see.

If this and that
can be true
don't you think
the same applies
to those dreams
you pursue?

— The Universe

The change
you have been wanting
is coming soon.
The visions
that filled your dreams
day and night
have been in tune
with a bigger picture
bestowed upon you
by the universe

— but will you trust it, too?

Vulnerability,
a scary place to be
in this world,
at least that's what they say.

Openly showing
your softer side
seen as a weakness,
so they all try to hide.

But when you embrace it
as part of you
and do so with pride,
you have no reason
to be terrified.

For it really is
your greatest strength.
A blessing in disguise,
there for you to recognize.

What If

All those stories
of great love and friendships
and yet
I haven't had any of them —
it makes you feel quite left out

but what if
maybe this still is
the universes way
of working things out
behind the scenes
while I'm standing here
with all my doubt.

What if
maybe all this time
of being alone
was to prepare me
for something greater
than I could ever imagine
sending me on a
different route.

What if
what once was
my greatest desire
will fulfill itself
in magical ways
and if I persisted
on doing things my way
I would be left
without.

What if
it's all leading me
to being my greatest self?
What if this moment
right now
is what it's all about?

All your desires
are rooted to the earth,
what you want
is what you deserve;
tap into this knowing
by raising your self worth.

Dare
to live life
in unconventional
ways
and be the witness
of all your concerns
vanishing
in a dusty haze.

Your full potential
may then come through,
no longer the person
you once knew
for much broader
your view will be;
a way of living
so joyfully
that you cannot
foresee.

"I don't know",
you said.
"How am I
supposed
to go about this?"
and
"What do I
have to bring to the table?",
you asked.
"There's nothing special
about me.
I have nothing to share
with the world",
you stated.

And yet,
here you are
beaming out
an energy
full of potential
full of healing
full of wisdom.

We think
it's about time
to go out
and share.

— The Universe

We don't
give guarantees.

But if you do it
because it feels good
we know
your life will be filled
with success.

— The Universe

Opportunities

And should you ever
find yourself
straying from your path
know that there are
many more roads
with the potentiality
to lead you to
where you want to be;
a thousand opportunities
for you in queue

— just trust and you will see.

YOUR TIME IS COMING
— AND COMING
SOON.

CAN'T YOU FEEL
IT APPROACHING,
AS THIS LAST PHASE
REACHES
IT'S COMPLETION,
JUST LIKE
A WAXING
MOON.

Trust
is what
we're asking for.
In return
you'll find
your wishes
fulfilled—
and more.

Sounds like a good deal,
right?

— The Universe

Every wish
you ever had
has been sent
like a letter
and this culmination
has created
the potential
for a future;

I've seen it,
so trust me
it will soon be
so much better.

— The Universe

A breakthrough is near
I can feel it within me,
deep inside my bones.
An intuitive wisdom
coming in clear;

piece my piece
the picture sharpens
still
no physical proof
only a knowing
but this time
I won't give in to fear;

this time I will trust,
that's how my desires will appear—
it is law
it must.

Faster than the wind
situations coming
flowing in,
your life
changing,
turning,
like a dime.
OH, WHAT WONDER!
It will feel
so divine.

RETURN BACK HOME

The Authority of You

Your own way
has to be found,
your own reality
has to be created.

No rigid structures,
no rule books
can ever entitle you
to this freedom.

Instead
take away all
the comfortable
and the uncomfortable
walls of laws
that you once
erected for yourself,
destroy them
if you ever want
to find peace
and a place to call
home
within yourself.

Let your guard down
I said,
beautiful things
want to make
their way to you
but you have to listen
if you want
to fulfill your mission

I see,
now you received
the transmission.

— The Universe

In the moments
where I feel like
I don't have enough
I stop
and remember
less is more
what is right now
is alright—
THIS MOMENT IS ENOUGH.

To: The Universe

All my life
knowing you were there
despite phases of denial,
and absolute despair.

You never left my side
even when I cried,
your energy always
in the air.

Followed by times
of joy and growth,
and I am wondering
did we go through them both?

Does it really exist,
the mirroring effect?
At least that's what I suspect.

My journey wasn't
all glitter and glow
but it was worth it,
now I know.

Eternal memories
crash into me,
colliding with
reality.
A tug of war until
I give up all control.
Now,
wisdom dawns
inside my soul:
the first time
I feel whole.

Walk in the Fog

All I remember
a sudden immersion
in gray nebulous clouds
nowhere an escape
to be found.

All I could see was confusion, my mind
caught up in the depths of delusion,
my mind went in circles
around.

Wish I would have noticed sooner
that it was me
who held the fog machine,
slowly turning up the intensity,
how blind I must have been;

But it's alright
for now I know
I don't have to keep picking up
this machine; now I know
what I prefer: to live life
in tune with my inner compass
trusting the universe's flow.

TAKING A
DEEP BREATH

ALL
THAT IS FILLING
MY CHEST—

LIFE'S WISDOM
IN DEPTH.

Nature's Music

To be outside in nature
is to listen closely to nature's music
so you might hear
the wind whisper
the wisdom of all
what was,
what is
and what soon
will be.

Let this moment fill you
with absolute clarity
and you may see
that at our core
we are all so very free.

Eternal
stretching out into the
endless
all that we are
feelings,
emotions,
thoughts
nothing is ever lost.

Infinite love is our home.

And I stopped resenting
all those
uncomfortable feelings
I had.
Instead
I started to accept
and embrace them
and suddenly
for the first time
I felt so free
like I had never been.

These feelings
were still inside of me
but turned
from being the enemy,
taking away all my air,
to a loving friend
giving me space
to be.

And it felt so good
when I could finally
breathe.

I Will Never Be The Same

Thank you
to all those who left me standing
in the cold—
I will never be the same,
now I'm so much more bold.
Thank you
to all those who broke my heart—
I will never be the same,
you lead me to create my art.
Thank you
to the times where everything turned
into gloomy shades of blue—
I will never be the same,
it gave me a higher view.
Thank you
to the people who chose to stay—
I will never be the same,
you make me believe in brighter days.
Thank you
to all these blessings that surely will continue
to enter my life—
I am happy
that things are always changing
and never stay the same.

And just when you thought
miracles don't exist
they happen.

We told you
it would be worth
the wait.

— The Universe

WHAT
I
FOUND

Once I thought
I was all on my own
but I never gave up,
never lost hope.
It's like I had known
on some larger scope
there soon would be
a way back up.

What I found:
if you're willing to look,
around every corner
is a helping hand,
a supportive friend
almost
heaven-sent.

TO SURRENDER
TO THE LOVER
YOU INHERENTLY ARE
IS TO LIVE
FROM A PLACE OF LOVE
AT ALL TIMES.

Send Love

Send love
to those who cared for you.
Send love
to those who saw the best in you.
Send love
to those close to your heart.

Also send love
to those who are no longer with you.
Send love
to those with whom your ways have parted.
Send love
even to those who left you scarred.
Send love
even to those who brought you tears
for they have helped you figure out
your boundaries,
now they're so much more clear.

Of life this is all an essential part,
so see the teacher
within all people you meet
and never close your heart.

Love is the medicine.
The power to heal
what no one can see
but you can feel.

Those who are close
to your heart,
love them deeply.
And you might soon see
a healing, so completely
that where once were scars,
you now find stars.

Heaven Parting

That feeling
when you found them.
The colleagues.
The friends.
The lovers.

Like heaven's parting?
Like angels singing?
Like the universe
giving you a handshake?

Pretty much
all of the above.

And the best thing?
The finding was just
the starting.

— The Universe

You are beauty
in all it's entirety;
all your flaws
all your scars
all your ability
all that makes up you
all that ties into your soul —

together
it paints you
whole.

The Earth Loves in Flowers

A wise man once said
the earth loves in flowers
and he is not wrong:

It loves in sunshines
and waterfalls,
in birds singing their tunes
and all those beautiful
sunlit moons.

It loves in cat purrs
and a dogs wagging tail,
in palm trees
and those beautiful
mountain trails.

The earth loves in flowers
and everything else
life on earth
entails.

Sun on skin
and my cells squeal with glee
lungs breathe fresh air
legs move along trail;
Oh what a joy
to simply be—
long exhale.

Things That Bring Me Joy

laughter sunshine and some tea;
the moments
where I feel absolutely free.

rainbows, sunflowers and a breeze;
anything that helps me
to be more at ease.

dancing, music and a smile;
all the times
where I forget the world
just for a while.

See this flower
how it blooms
small, thin and
vulnerable.

See that tree
how it stands
tall, massive and
stable.

Together
they want you
to be aware
that strength and beauty
are not defined
by size or appearance.

Strength and Beauty
can be found
deep within you.
It can be seen
in how you carry your heart
out into the world,
love always
in the background.

So instead of striving
for perfection in your looks,
reach for alignment
with your soul
then you'll feel it
within you

— You have always been whole.

My Wish For Us All

I look up
at the stars at night
and there I see
a shooting star;
so I wish
for us all to realize
that who we are
is light and love;
our true essence,
always near
and never far.

Appreciation for
the simplest things.
Not taking for granted,
and instead being enchanted
by the beauty
of the ever unfolding process
called life.

Abundance

A never ending
stream of experiences;
that's like abundance.

An overarching
theme of choices and free will;
that is abundance.

More than you can dream
by being relaxed and chill;
that's where you'll find
abundance.

Sunshine
creeping in
through the window.
All I see,
a golden glow.
An energy
so warming.
It's surrounding
my whole being.
Suddenly
everything around me
I'm now seeing
through different eyes:
love.

An Ode to Life

Oh! magic, bliss, love — truly
wonderful states
to be in
and how easily
you can access them.

Oh! nature, meditation,
each and every experience
you make,
holding infinite potential
to feel good
by choosing
to feel just a little better.

See
how life can be
a never-ending
love letter?

A Place to Call Home

I found love in the seeds
I planted within myself
all those years ago.

Wasn't sure
where this would lead me to,
but I'm glad I did;
my expectation's overflown.

'Cause
now on the horizon
I see a golden glow,
now within me emerges
a place to call home.

ENERGY IS BOUNDLESS,

KNOWS NO LIMITS.

THERE ARE NO BORDERS

THAT CAN KEEP IT CONTAINED

AND NOT ENOUGH WORDS

FOR IT TO EVER BE EXPLAINED.

Go on.
The time to act,
it's now.

Speak up.
Tell them the truth.
You are here
to help them wake up.

It's time for you
to let your gifts
shine through.

— The Universe

FINDING HOME

And after months
and months of rain;
after all the thoughts
that you safely
replayed in your head
and after all the secrets
that you kept
now it's time to look ahead
as the sunshine creeps back in;
now all the thoughts that once
have been trapped
are ready to be expressed
and there's no more reason
to be afraid or stressed
because you're no longer alone;
now you have support
you can always lean on

— YOU'VE FINALLY FOUND HOME.

ABOUT THE AUTHOR

KJ is a poet and spiritual seeker who is channeling the universe through her work. Her writings cover themes such as hope, love, healing and more. She also works as an online Reiki Energy Healer.

Her debut poetry collection *Conversations with The Universe* features channeled messages from the universe on topics such as faith, trust, inner peace and finding a new sense of purpose in life.

When she isn't writing, doing energy work or conversing with the Universe, you can find her on long nature walks with her dog, on her yoga mat, watching a sunset or traveling the world.

www.kjrobinsonpoetry.com
@kj.robinsonpoetry on Instagram
@kjrobinsonpoetry on TikTok

Covversations with the Universe

ISBN: 978-3-00-073443-4 (paperback),
978-3-00-073444-1 (ebook),
978-3-00-073535-6 (hardback).

Book Design & Layout by Rachel Clift. rcliftpoetry.com

First printing edition, 2022.

K. J. Robinson
@kj.robinsonpoetry

CPSIA information can be obtained
at www.ICGtesting.com
Printed in the USA
LVHW070859181022
730943LV00014B/736